The World
of
Risk Management

Roles, Personality Traits, Talents,
Awareness and Issues of the Risk Manager

by
Bill Kizorek and George Ushiba

PSI
PUBLICATIONS

1163 E. Ogden Avenue • Suite 705-360
Naperville, Illinois 60563
(708) 955-0940

Produced and Designed by Nikki Lincoln
Illustrated by Al Ochsner

Printed in Singapore

Library of Congress Cataloging-in-Publication Data

Kizorek, Bill
The world of risk management / by Bill Kizorek and George Ushiba;
[illustrated by Al Ochsner].
p.   cm.
ISBN 1-884230-04-0
1. Risk management. I. Ushiba, Yasuhiko, 1937—   .   II. Title
HD61.K59   1996
658.4--dc20   96-1549
CIP

Table of Contents

Credits

Thanks to George Ushiba without whose constant communication and knowledge this book would not have been written. Scott Finger (my co-author for SIU 101) applied such heavy editing that he almost qualified as a co-author. Carly Kizorek spent long hours laying out the pages, and Janie Kizorek provided continued support (I continue a decade-long, nepotistic tradition). Steve Wall was brutally frank and Jean Dever was always there faxing back and forth to Tokyo. Eight thousand clients from all sectors of the claims and risk management sectors influenced the thinking in this book.

I am not formally trained in risk management. A decade-long relationship with some of the industry leaders, especially in a vendor/client relationship, has allowed me to make conclusions about what I felt were the qualities pertinent to success in the world of risk management. Without the friendship of these executives, I would not have had the insight to produce this book. Special thanks go to Phil Palazzo, Doug Lawson, Ken Morrissey, Dick Willie, Ken Coy, and Ron Bokowy. Hank Greenberg has been a significant influence on the production of this book because of the long-term access I have had to high-level executives within his company.

序　文

この本は、見た目にはシンプルに映るかもしれません。
でも、リスク・マネジメントの題材を幾度となく注意深く
再吟味し、５年の歳月をついやして完成したものです。
たくさんの事実を十分に煮つめたのちに、ジョージ・ウシバと
私は、我々二人が感じていることこそ、リスク・マネジメント
世界の本質だとの結論に達しました。

リスク・マネジメントは複雑多岐にわたる仕事です。
そして　この分野のことは、さらにもっと多くの本に書かれ
たら良いと思います。
この本から学んでいただくと同時に大いに楽しんでいただければ
幸いです。

ビル　キゾーレック

Introduction

This book may appear simple on the surface,
but it is the result of five years of effort and
review of thousands of pages of risk management material.
After boiling off a few tons of facts,
George Ushiba and I have come up with what
we feel is the essence of the risk management world.

Risk management is a complex profession
and much more could have been written.
This book's contents, however,
should amuse as well as educate.

Bill Kizorek

ま　え　が　き

私が　リスク・マネジメントを始めてから２５年が経ちました。
この間、このテーマに関する本をたくさん書いてきました。
たいへん嬉しいことに、このたび、インフォト・サベイランス社の
ビル・キゾーレック社長から一緒に本を書いてみないかとのお誘い
を受けました。
この本を書くにあたって、我々二人は、幼児からお年寄りまで
幅広い読者を対象とすることにしました。　そして　この本を
ユーモアに満ち、ウイットに富む楽しいものにしようといろいろと
工夫をこらしました。　各ページには美しいカラーのさし絵を入れ、
リスク・マネジャーの役割や資質などに関し、できるだけやさしく
書くことに努めました。

リスク・マネジメントはアメリカの保険の分野で誕生しました。
率直に申して、私の住んでいる日本は残念なことに未だこの道では
ごく初期の段階にあります。このため、これまでわれわれ日本人は
リスク・マネジメントに関して多くのことをアメリカや西洋の国々
から学んできました。

しかし東洋にも数千年に及ぶ長い歴史があります。　そこで、西洋で
発達している秀れた技法に、東洋の知恵をプラスしてより良いリスク・
マネジメントを創りあげることができれば、すばらしいことではない
でしょうか。

アメリカやヨーロッパの方々のみならず、この本が日本をはじめとして
東洋の国々の読者にも広く読んでいただければと念じております。

牛場靖彦

Preface

Twenty-five years have already elapsed since I began to handle risk management. During these years, I have written many books on this theme. To my great joy, this time, I was requested by Mr. Bill Kizorek, the president of InPhoto Surveillance, to co-author this book. We decided the book should be comprehensible to readers from very young children to the aged. Also, we took efforts to make the book enjoyable with wit and humor. The artwork throughout the book helps explain the roles and personalities of risk managers.

Risk management was born in the insurance field of the U.S.A. To be frank, unfortunately, it is still in the infant stage in Japan (where I live). Therefore, we Japanese have been learning many things from the U.S.A. and the Western countries regarding risk management.

However, we, the Far East people have long histories of more than a few thousand years. So, I think it is better to adopt some wisdom of the Orient into risk management techniques that has developed in the Western countries.

I earnestly wish our performance is well-received by the readers throughout the world, not only those in the U.S.A. and European countries, but also the readers in Japan and throughout the Far East.

Y. Ushiba

The book is dedicated to all risk managers.
I had some inkling about how important
they were prior to commencing this book.
Now, as my work is done,
I realize that they are downright indispensable.

B.K.

Roles

The risk manager wears many hats. Not every risk manager has the same responsibilities, but there are similar roles which most of them play.

Risk Identifier

Accidents happen. But they should not happen in the future with the same frequency as in the past. Risk managers need to be on the alert for where yesterday's banana peels were slipped on and where tomorrow's peels may fall.

Guardian

Worrying is not enough. A risk manager is the primary guardian of resources. That guardianship is manifested in recognizing the location of the most important corporate assets---whether they be offices or operating rooms---and putting into place the appropriate fiscal protections.

Renaissance Man

Or woman. Being versatile and creative is a must during the normal course of business, especially if that business is in the midst of a reconstruction or renewal.

Worrier

The risk manager is the official corporate worrier, whose job is to think of all the things that might impact the welfare and survival of the organization.

Crisis Manager

Risk managers are not only dealing with potential future risks. They are often involved ex-post-facto and mucho pronto in a crisis that happened four hours ago.

Convincer

Speaking skills are essential to the risk manager. The job demands that the manager meet with many big bosses as well as convey information critical to the welfare of legions of employees. Listening to those legions is often helpful.

Trainer

To reduce losses, lower the incidence of claims, enhance safety and increase overall awareness of these issues, the risk manager takes on the role of corporate trainer. Through memos, meetings, job-site visits, and audiovisual training tools, the risk manager alerts employees to the issues of risk.

Problem Solver

A risk manager is not usually a rat. But sometimes there are mazes to be worked through before the answers are found; and, at times, there is something like stinky cheese that needs to be removed from the maze.

Researcher

A risk manager is always researching---looking for better ways of doing things---comparing past events to future plans---cutting a path to control losses and increase profits. Reducing risk is almost always more desirable than transferring it.

Organizer

A risk manager is also an organizer. In Japan, the cormorant-handler catches fish with cormorants. Each cormorant is tethered, and a hook is put round its neck in order to prevent it from swallowing the fish it catches.

Intelligence Officer

The risk manager must be a part-time secret agent to spot industry trends and stay aware of what the competition is doing. This helps prevent losses, lawsuits, injuries, and accidents.

And, to round it out, the Risk Manager should have a: Hunger for Knowledge

Risk management is not a stagnant job. It is not inert. To stay on top of global developments, the risk manager must constantly be devouring the latest information. Current information is a valuable risk management tool. Staying current is staying successful.

Personality Traits, Talents

Some risk managers have been enormously successful, others have not. Although random bad luck has "done in" a few risk management careers, many professionals have found fulfillment in this discipline. Following are some personality traits and talents that a risk manager will find helpful in dealing with the day-to-day travail of managing risk.

Open-Minded

Keeping a balanced perspective is important---listening to all sectors of the organization, then making decisions which best serve the company as a whole.

Philosophical

Stuff happens. Disasters destroy. Catastrophe and calamity are part of life. Claims will be filed; losses will occur. All the risk manager can do is plan as thoroughly as possible. When dealing with an eventual problem, a manager with a philosophical levelheadedness will help keep others calm and save them from becoming immobilized. Proper planning will reduce confusion and cut costs.

Political Proficiency

The risk manager is often poking around in the bailiwick of others. Some organizations have department heads who are "protective" of their realms. In order to get the job done, a risk manager may, at times, need the skills of a politician so that not too many ruffled feathers fill the air.

Balance

そば

The employee of the soba (Japanese noodle) shop is well trained and cool-headed to carry a pile of bricks or steaming bowls on his shoulder while often riding a bicycle. There are times risk managers need to do many complicated things at the same time.

Vision

Predicting the unpredictable. Preparing for uncertainty. And your own future depends upon how successful you are at doing so. Nice job! Anyone want to apply?

Proactive

The risk manager cannot react to events. Managing is not simply a defensive position. The position demands one to be dynamic in many settings and act early instead of reacting late.

A Knack for Measurement

A risk manager is a quantifier and measurer. Benchmarking, seeing what the industry leaders are doing, and comparing performance is vital. Also important is relating these findings to internal and external statistics.

Innovative

Ancient kite flyer's proverb: "He who never fly kite in storm never get hit by lightening bolt." There are times that the risk manager must be entrepreneurial and experimental. An intermittent jolt may occur, but new discoveries (and savings) may justify the experiment.

Coordinating

The risk manager runs from department to department, coordinating company-wide policies. At times you get one of those pieces that is supposed to fit in, but...

Motivational

A true art. What great philosopher said honey was better than a hammer? Some risk managers must be agreeably disagreeable and use a full range of people skills to accomplish what might appear to be the simplest of goals.

Directional

No lights or cameras, but lots of actors and action. A risk manager needs to transform much of the organization's strategy into reality by taking the screenplay and working for an Oscar instead of a farce.

And like the Tibetan Deity, *Chenrezi*

There once was a Tibetan deity by the name of Chenrezi. He had a thousand arms and multiple heads so he could better think about and handle problems. Perhaps he was also the Tibetan god of risk management?

Awareness

It would be fun to operate in a vacuum (not the kind filled with floor dirt, but the one that is quiet, windless, and pure). But the risk manager operates in a real world filled with competitors, government, employees, bosses, clients, vendors, and other assorted (or distorted) distractions. As risk managers go about their daily business, there are a variety of issues to pay attention to, including but certainly not limited to...

Acquisitions

Why be aware of a soon-to-be-purchased baby formula factory recently built on the same foundation as a dismantled Russian plutonium reactor? OOPS, did they forget to tell the v.p. of acquisitions about the recent recall of sixty-five million pallets of formula from Inner Mongolia? Did anyone even ask?

Knowledge of Government Regs

OK, how about knowledge of some of the laws? Some losses arise out of violations of government regulations. And we aren't just talking about the obvious ones; for instance, paying income taxes. How about something like the ADA section 3, part 161, subchapter B, code 4a relating to the fiber content of lunch for a disabled milk cow? It's not so bad if it is just one cow, but if you've been feeding 2,000 cows the wrong stuff for nine years, you had better check up on the coverage in those older general liability policies. Don't forget planning future building layout and "reasonable accommodations."

Exposure

Risk managers have to be aware of potential losses because of some contingency, way of doing things, or other hazard. And each year brings new "trends" such as sexual harassment, wrongful discharge, and injuries such as repetitive stress trauma.

Cultural Awareness

If a risk manager has a total of three plants in one state, cultural awareness may not be a big issue. But a risk manager dealing with thousands of employees across the world should have insights into the more obvious regional differences.

Focus Locally,

Think Globally

Should the risk manager of Podunk Pretzel of Pennsylvania prognosticate about pretzel processing in Portugal? It is not critical, but following global issues on safety, manufacturing, and other issues will give your organization a "leg up" on the competition. This is also why risk managers should attend international risk management conferences in Australia, Monte Carlo, and Singapore.

Knowledge of Laws

What's the problem? There are only twenty million or so laws. Just be aware of the three or four million which, if violated by one of the employees of your firm, might end up as the dominant reason your company had to pay out ninety million pesos in a court award.

Surveillance

There are times the risk manager uses investigators (usually outside vendors) to help out with problems like worker's compensation, disability, or fraud. Surveillance is an effective tool and is legal as long as investigators understand risk management themselves and realize that the subjects of the investigation have a "reasonable expectation of privacy." As this book went to press, a federal court in Wyoming ordered a claimant to pay back Northwestern Mutual Insurance $971,000 because a surveillance showed he was not as disabled as he alleged.

The Environment

Air, water, earth, pollution. Deciding when to buy environmental impairment insurance might cause mental impairment.

Staying In Business

European risk manager Hugh Loader said it: "The real issue is to stay in business; companies (and countries) cannot afford to lose resources, which is what every loss/claim does. Think of a matchstick mountain: gradually there are none left."

Frivolous Suits

Not to be confused with leisure suits, which are now out of vogue with most civilized risk managers. More risk managers are standing up to "nuisance suits," even if they cost more to defend than settle. Some are countersuing. Although defending frivolous suits may cost more in the beginning, the company's reputation for not being a "soft touch" should, in the long run, pay dividends.

Risk History

History repeats itself. Isn't that the reason for experience modifiers?
To accurately position current risk management resources and funds,
it is critical to recognize the dangers and losses of the past.

Reserving

A loss occurs. So what's it worth to you? Reserving is one of those educated guessing games played with a bunch of "what if" pieces, setting aside funds to pay for losses. A risk manager's possible reserve calculation session: "OK, the demand on this claim is fourteen million. The last time we went to trial on a similar case we paid out seven million. But I can settle this for seventy thousand."

Change Management

Just as tires wear out and become useless, so do contracts, vendors, insurers, policies, and laws. The risk manager has got to be willing to get dirty hands by replacing what does not work with what does, all the while remembering what Machiavelli said about change: "It is the only constant."

While keeping an eye on all this stuff, Don't Forget Mahatma Gandhi.

Gandhi's Advice:

As the risk manager tries to allocate the protective resources of the company, it is important to be vigilant of those who would try to take more than they deserve. In the area of claims, especially in the USA, there is not enough money in any corporate treasury to pay all the demands. Keep in mind the risk management advice from Mahatma Gandhi, who said, "The world contains enough for every man's need, but not enough for every man's greed."

Issues

Each day new concerns about the management of risk pop up. Many are specific issues requiring quick action. At other times the risk manager has the luxury of dealing with broader issues of a more general nature. As the risk manager grapples with some of these issues, it might be wise to keep in mind the words of Albert Einstein: "Out of clutter find simplicity; from discord make harmony; in the middle of difficulty lies opportunity." Here are some places to find clutter, discord, and difficulty.

The Insurer

Sometimes a "great deal" on premiums is not so hot when the time comes (seven years later) to pay the claim. One or two risk managers have found themselves in the "hot seat" by saving a little too much money on the premium side of the deal.

Statistic Gathering

Whether forecasting future needs or tracking past losses, the risk manager needs numbers. Loss runs. Details. Statistics fuel those great actuarial "bean counting and prediction" machines. Caution: don't compare apples to oranges.

Disaster Recovery Planning

Sure they call the risk manager at 2:00 a.m. when the train carrying 60 tankers of cyanide catapults off a bridge into Lake Superior. But who does the bleary-eyed risk ruler call? Disaster recovery is planned in advance with tricks-of-the-trade such as phone trees. One call from the risk manager can activate hundreds of phone calls.

Surprising a CFO

If you can help it, don't.

Risk Transfer or Retention

One theory: if the loss is predictable, retain the risk. The more unpredictable, the greater the need to buy insurance (from those who might be more adept at predicting a loss or have big enough shoulders to survive a scourge).

Industrial Hygiene

Sometimes there are safety managers. Sometimes there aren't. If the risk manager is buying insurance, the insurer wants to see the "loss runs." Who got hurt? Where? How many times? The safer an operation, the cheaper the insurance. There are times to put on the risk management hard hat and attack.

Vendor Management

Even the most self-sufficient organizations need outside help. In the risk management business many of those helpers are generically referred to as vendors. Although vendor dealings can sometimes be akin to pest control, efficient vendors (TPA's, investigators, brokers) will simplify and enhance the business life of a risk manager, as well as add value to the risk manager's organization. Trust, integrity, innovation, flexibility, and long-term commitment are some of the symbiotic things to look for in the relationship.

Risk Elimination

福は内！
(Fortune in)

鬼は外！
(Devil out)

A risk manager always pays his attention to eliminate risks. In Japan, SETSUBUN, or Bean-Throwing Ceremony, is held on February 3rd every year. The Grand Champion SUMO wrestler throws a handful of parched beans, crying, "Devil Out!" Although risk managers don't have to be as beefy as sumo guys, they still might have to throw out beans once in a while or at least try to eliminate risks which "bedevil" their company.

Zombie-Zapping

There are those in any organization who are practically brain dead. Their mindless actions are a hazard to the survival of the organization. Risk managers must be alert to the hazards zombies can cause, identify where they are, and act accordingly.
(George Ushiba travels throughout Asia lecturing on this theme.)

And, above all, not forgetting about the
Big Picture

Risk managers are not in outer space. Nor should they be spacey or spaced out. But they should be (at times) far enough away from the rumble of the boiler room to have an overview of the operations.

About Author Bill Kizorek

Bill Kizorek is the author of 8 books on surveillance, investigations, testifying and risk management. He is the president of InPhoto Surveillance and a consultant to the claims industry. Bill has lectured on six continents and been to over 100 countries. He has also appeared on national and international television shows such as 20/20, Inside Edition, Dateline N.B.C., Oprah, A.M. Singapore, and London Weekend T.V.

About Author George Ushiba

George Ushiba is the president of Ushiba International Office (a risk management consultancy) and president of the International Risk Management Society of Japan (IRMS-J). He is the author of 44 books on risk management and sumo wrestling, and an officer of the International Federation of Risk and Insurance Management Association (IFRIMA).

About the Illustrator
Al Ochsner

This effort marks the 6th collaborative book published with InPhoto's Bill Kizorek for Al Ochsner. Despite two degrees in painting from Western Michigan University and The School of the Art Institute of Chicago, Al calls more upon his sophomoric skills perfected as a 6th grade class clown to inspire his illustrative abilities. He can generally be found creating some art project without shoes at any time of the day or year.